THE ID

THE
IDENTITY
JOURNAL

A PERSONAL ACCOUNT OF YOURSELF WRITTEN TO YOURSELF

THE IDENTITY JOURNAL

A PERSONAL ACCOUNT OF YOURSELF
WRITTEN TO YOURSELF

Copyright © 2018 by Dr. Sonny Alonzo Dotson

All rights reserved

A Product of:
OmniOne Books
OmniOne Publishing, LLC
OmniOne Publishing Direct
Please Visit:

www.drsonnyalonzodotson.com
www.sadminc.com
or
www.sadotsonenterprises.com
for further information or services

THE IDENTITY JOURNAL

This Identity Journal is in the rightful possession of:

Date I decided to start discovering the truth about myself:

THE IDENTITY JOURNAL

Introduction

This journal is an experience of total oneness with self. It a form of self expression that is based on the ability to tell yourself the truth. It is a place and a platform that acts as refuge from falsification and fabrication of self. It is a home away from the needs and expectations of society and social norms and/or normalcy. It is home to where questioning, and then answering yourself is possible. We need to know who we are and the truth surrounding our identity. We need to come to terms with the self-acceptance we do so deserve. In this identity journal no one is judging you for who you grew up and became. No one is judging you about whats seemingly controversial or socially unacceptable. You will remain free to be truly who you are and be totally fine with that. In this journal, you don't owe anyone any excuses for how you feel or how you choose to live your life day to day. It is your life you know! In this journal, no one has the right to tell you what career to choose. Who or what to be. No one has the right to tell you what car to drive. No one has the right to tell you what house or neighborhood to reside in. You don't owe anyone an explanation about your gender choice. About your sexual identity. About who you have made the decision to love. What religion to choose. Who you choose to identify as. What race you are and so on and so on. Why? Because every day when you choose to pick up this identity journal and begin to talk to yourself about yourself, you have chose to make your own decision about your life. That right! YOUR LIFE! No one but you. You my dear friend are someone special. You every dream and hearts desire and so much more. You are so great and so awesome. And now, its time for someone else to start building trust in the truth of who you are, whatever that is. Besides me. Laughing out loud. No seriously. In this identity journal there will be tons of questions you will be answering about yourself. No, this is not one of those 365 day so on and so on. It doesn't matter when you pick up this journal. It is yours to keep, remember? You just jot down when and where you are and begin answering yourself. Speaking back to yourself and begin telling your own self why. With this journal, you are basically demanding an answer from your own psyche. Not the most often shrewd opinions of others. Not saying other people are not great and all but you know exactly what I'm talking about. Here, you are not in any competition with anyone or anything. This is exploration of self and the identity that encompasses it. In this identity journal, you are beginning everyday with loving yourself just a tiny winy bit more. Your are taking back the right to your own body and the power of your own thoughts. You are building trust within yourself that you've never experienced before. You are listen to your body, mind, heart, and spirit that lies deep within. Every single thing you write is getting you one step closer to oneness with self and the truth about yourself that you have been hiding from for however long you have been hiding. No one knows you are doing this and who cares, so stop beating yourself down already and lets begin the self-discovery process. Lets begin providing an answer to ourselves and the questions of our hearts. Talk back to yourself!

THE IDENTITY JOURNAL

Before you begin journaling

Proclaim these Affirmations out loud.......

Say this 10 times

I AM

WORTHY	WELL
HEALTHY	WHOLE

THE IDENTITY JOURNAL

What's up next?

Self-Concept & Self-Reflection

Turn the page and stop staring at it.

THE IDENTITY JOURNAL

What day of the week is it?

What date and time is it?

Where am I?

What am I thinking right now in this very moment?

What are you looking at right in front of you?

What do I believe about myself right now?

THE IDENTITY JOURNAL

What day of the week is it?

What date and time is it?

Where am I?

Who am I really?

No, really, who am I cause I don't know?

Am I really aware of my worthiness? Cause I don't feel worthy

THE IDENTITY JOURNAL

What day of the week is it?

What date and time is it?

Where am I?

**Do I love myself today?
Answer me**

THE IDENTITY JOURNAL

What day of the week is it?

What date and time is it?

Where am I?

What is the full sum of me and my character?

THE IDENTITY JOURNAL

What day of the week is it?

What date and time is it?

Where am I?

What is my Identity and what am I here for on this planet called earth?

THE IDENTITY JOURNAL

What day of the week is it?

What date and time is it?

Where am I?

Who do I want to be and who am I becoming?

THE IDENTITY JOURNAL

What day of the week is it?

What date and time is it?

Where am I?

What do I want out of life and do I deserve it?

THE IDENTITY JOURNAL

What day of the week is it?

What date and time is it?

Where am I?

Am I living under the agony of self distortion?

THE IDENTITY JOURNAL

What day of the week is it?

What date and time is it?

Where am I?

Am I my number one priority?

THE IDENTITY JOURNAL

What day of the week is it?

What date and time is it?

Where am I?

Am I full of ego or the pseudo-self mission?

THE IDENTITY JOURNAL

What day of the week is it?

What date and time is it?

Where am I?

Am I full of foolish pride?

THE IDENTITY JOURNAL

What day of the week is it?

What date and time is it?

Where am I?

Am I empty on the inside?

THE IDENTITY JOURNAL

What day of the week is it?

What date and time is it?

Where am I?

Do you ever feel lost and don't know which way is left or right anymore?

THE IDENTITY JOURNAL

What day of the week is it?

What date and time is it?

Where am I?

Are you a kind and generous person?

THE IDENTITY JOURNAL

What day of the week is it?

What date and time is it?

Where am I?

What do you care about most?

THE IDENTITY JOURNAL

What day of the week is it?

What date and time is it?

Where am I?

What are my deepest darkest secrets?

THE IDENTITY JOURNAL

What day of the week is it?

What date and time is it?

Where am I?

Who and what am I currently hiding from?

THE IDENTITY JOURNAL

What day of the week is it?

What date and time is it?

Where am I?

What do I loathe most about myself?

THE IDENTITY JOURNAL

What day of the week is it?

What date and time is it?

Where am I?

What do I enjoy most about myself?

THE IDENTITY JOURNAL

What day of the week is it?

What date and time is it?

Where am I?

What am I currently believing about myself that were the lies of others?

THE IDENTITY JOURNAL

What day of the week is it?

What date and time is it?

Where am I?

Do you feel loneliness all the time?

THE IDENTITY JOURNAL

What day of the week is it?

What date and time is it?

Where am I?

Am I really coping through life or do I just hate my darn self?

THE IDENTITY JOURNAL

What day of the week is it?

What date and time is it?

Where am I?

Gee, I feel extremely happy today! Do you?

What day of the week is it?

What date and time is it?

Where am I?

What is the story that I am telling myself each and every single day?

THE IDENTITY JOURNAL

What day of the week is it?

What date and time is it?

Where am I?

Am I still suffering from the bondage of my past?

THE IDENTITY JOURNAL

What day of the week is it?

What date and time is it?

Where am I?

What do you long for in the long term considering your life?

What the heck is next this time?
Oh I know!

> **Just Perfect!**
> **Those good ole' Affirmations**
>
> **Speak these affirmations proudly into the atmosphere**
>
> **Say each one a total of 20 times**

Affirmations to Exclaim aloud:

I am peace

I am love

I am ever changing

I am one with my Identity

I am one with who I have chosen to be

I am the full product of my own decisions

I am relying on my own thought processes

I am willing to forgive myself

I am willing to start rebuilding any trust that has been lost during the years of my past experiences

I am understanding of my needs and care about my overall welfare

I am building and creating new visions about myself again

I am leaving the expectations of my ego and the fabrication of my pseudo-self

I am trying

I am making steps

I am taking leaps!

THE IDENTITY JOURNAL

Hey again!

Well, what's next you may be asking?

Woven Behavior Patterns

What day of the week is it?

What date and time is it?

Where am I?

What negative patterns and behavior am I still holding on to that are believed to be getting me through life?

THE IDENTITY JOURNAL

What day of the week is it?

What date and time is it?

Where am I?

Am I living in insanity?

THE IDENTITY JOURNAL

What day of the week is it?

What date and time is it?

Where am I?

What is my patterned behavior day to day? Am I satisfied?

THE IDENTITY JOURNAL

What day of the week is it?

What date and time is it?

Where am I?

Am I a competitive person?

THE IDENTITY JOURNAL

What day of the week is it?

What date and time is it?

Where am I?

When you speak your full name aloud, how do you feel? Are you proud?

THE IDENTITY JOURNAL

What day of the week is it?

What date and time is it?

Where am I?

What is at the core of the beliefs that I have about myself?

THE IDENTITY JOURNAL

What day of the week is it?

What date and time is it?

Where am I?

How do I currently define my personality?

THE IDENTITY JOURNAL

What day of the week is it?

What date and time is it?

Where am I?

Who am I seeing when I gaze into my mirror and see the reflection shining back at me?

THE IDENTITY JOURNAL

What day of the week is it?

What date and time is it?

Where am I?

How do I feel about myself when I am angry?

THE IDENTITY JOURNAL

What day of the week is it?

What date and time is it?

Where am I?

What is my natural mood?

THE IDENTITY JOURNAL

What day of the week is it?

What date and time is it?

Where am I?

It's so hard for me to get motivated about anything. What motivates you?

THE IDENTITY JOURNAL

What day of the week is it?

What date and time is it?

Where am I?

Talk to me please. Why do I feel so aggressive?

THE IDENTITY JOURNAL

What day of the week is it?

What date and time is it?

Where am I?

Somehow I am unable to express myself well today. Am I assertive enough?

THE IDENTITY JOURNAL

What day of the week is it?

What date and time is it?

Where am I?

By the way that I choose to express myself, who and what am I attracting with my energy?

THE IDENTITY JOURNAL

What day of the week is it?

What date and time is it?

Where am I?

Am I a passive person?

THE IDENTITY JOURNAL

What day of the week is it?

What date and time is it?

Where am I?

Am I unable to fully depend on myself ?

THE IDENTITY JOURNAL

What day of the week is it?

What date and time is it?

Where am I?

Can you tell me what my thoughts, needs, wants, and expectations of myself are?

THE IDENTITY JOURNAL

What day of the week is it?

What date and time is it?

Where am I?

Are you repetitive in your approach to life?

THE IDENTITY JOURNAL

What day of the week is it?

What date and time is it?

Where am I?

Am I an optimistic or pessimistic person? Is either one working for me?

THE IDENTITY JOURNAL

What day of the week is it?

What date and time is it?

Where am I?

Am I envious of other people's lives?

THE IDENTITY JOURNAL

What day of the week is it?

What date and time is it?

Where am I?

Do I have an unidentified personality disorder? Or am I just coping to get by?

THE IDENTITY JOURNAL

What day of the week is it?

What date and time is it?

Where am I?

Today I have came into the awareness about myself that....

THE IDENTITY JOURNAL

What day of the week is it?

What date and time is it?

Where am I?

Today I love myself because.....

THE IDENTITY JOURNAL

Oh Gosh!

It's what the heck is next again

yikes!

It's Affirmation time!

On the very next page after the next. Funny right? There will be affirmations to speak to yourself in total silence

While listening to what is around you, begin to speak the affirmations to yourself

Say them to yourself 30 times

Say them until they are planted in your consciousness

Your Identity matters!

Well, well, well

I know, you want to keep staring at this page trying to figure out if you should start doing something presumably more thrilling, right?

You just get to turning this page here!

Say these Affirmation 30 times in silence to yourself

I am present in my body

I am exploring who I am as a person, a real person, not some made up self expression of who everything and everyone else wants me to be

I am vibrant

I am resilient

I am self-serving

I am finding myself and loving who I am becoming as a human being

I deserve to be here

I am not strange nor weird

I am the best version of myself in the making

I am healing the wounds of my past

I am improving the relationship that I have with myself

I am present in my mind

I am present in my heart

I am honoring myself today and everyday forward

I am here

THE IDENTITY JOURNAL

Time for what's next again!

This time its personal!

Funny Right!

> Personal
> Qualities
> Individuality
> Relationships
> &
> Gender

THE IDENTITY JOURNAL

What day of the week is it?

What date and time is it?

Where am I?

Self, what are my best personal qualities and characteristics?

THE IDENTITY JOURNAL

What day of the week is it?

What date and time is it?

Where am I?

How am I communicating with myself daily? Is it healthy?

THE IDENTITY JOURNAL

What day of the week is it?

What date and time is it?

Where am I?

Am I working sufficiently with the gifts and talents that I possess?

THE IDENTITY JOURNAL

What day of the week is it?

What date and time is it?

Where am I?

Are you determined to excel in who you are as a person?

THE IDENTITY JOURNAL

What day of the week is it?

What date and time is it?

Where am I?

Am I living each day being fully honest about who I am?

THE IDENTITY JOURNAL

What day of the week is it?

What date and time is it?

Where am I?

Self, I am in harmony and unison with the energies I possess. Are you?

THE IDENTITY JOURNAL

What day of the week is it?

What date and time is it?

Where am I?

Are you happy when spending time alone with yourself?

THE IDENTITY JOURNAL

What day of the week is it?

What date and time is it?

Where am I?

Who am I as an individual? Do I currently have an individuality of mine own?

THE IDENTITY JOURNAL

What day of the week is it?

What date and time is it?

Where am I?

Am I one with my uniqueness?

THE IDENTITY JOURNAL

What day of the week is it?

What date and time is it?

Where am I?

What is my originality and where does it come from?

THE IDENTITY JOURNAL

What day of the week is it?

What date and time is it?

Where am I?

Am I right now able to recognize my separateness?

What day of the week is it?

What date and time is it?

Where am I?

How can you define your spiritual existence as it relates to your relationship with yourself?

THE IDENTITY JOURNAL

What day of the week is it?

What date and time is it?

Where am I?

Do you have a clear understanding of what distinguishes you from the likes of other people?

THE IDENTITY JOURNAL

What day of the week is it?

What date and time is it?

Where am I?

Tell me my attributes. What are they?

THE IDENTITY JOURNAL

What day of the week is it?

What date and time is it?

Where am I?

How is my relationship with myself today? Really?

THE IDENTITY JOURNAL

What day of the week is it?

What date and time is it?

Where am I?

How am I connecting on a deeper level with myself today?

THE IDENTITY JOURNAL

What day of the week is it?

What date and time is it?

Where am I?

How are my current and past relationships with other people?

THE IDENTITY JOURNAL

What day of the week is it?

What date and time is it?

Where am I?

How am I experiencing the affections of myself and others?

THE IDENTITY JOURNAL

What day of the week is it?

What date and time is it?

Where am I?

Am I spending the necessary time with myself to learn my communication issues?

THE IDENTITY JOURNAL

What day of the week is it?

What date and time is it?

Where am I?

Who and what am I attracted to?

THE IDENTITY JOURNAL

What day of the week is it?

What date and time is it?

Where am I?

What is my gender identification? How is it affecting my personal, private, and professional life

THE IDENTITY JOURNAL

What day of the week is it?

What date and time is it?

Where am I?

Am I freely breathing with my authenticity?

THE IDENTITY JOURNAL

What day of the week is it?

What date and time is it?

Where am I?

What is my personal experience of my gender?

THE IDENTITY JOURNAL

What day of the week is it?

What date and time is it?

Where am I?

Am I living behind the restrictions of my social identity? If so, why am I?

THE IDENTITY JOURNAL

What day of the week is it?

What date and time is it?

Where am I?

Self, are you able to accept me for exactly who I am experiencing myself to be at this moment?

THE IDENTITY JOURNAL

What day of the week is it?

What date and time is it?

Where am I?

I am one with my gender, identity, and self expression because I am freeing myself of self-hate. Self, are you?

THE IDENTITY JOURNAL

What day of the week is it?

What date and time is it?

Where am I?

Am I a beacon of light and hope for myself and others?

THE IDENTITY JOURNAL

What day of the week is it?

What date and time is it?

Where am I?

Am I accepting of others and their representation of their best self?

THE IDENTITY JOURNAL

What day of the week is it?

What date and time is it?

Where am I?

In what ways do other people classify and misinterpret me?

THE IDENTITY JOURNAL

What day of the week is it?

What date and time is it?

Where am I?

What opinions of others regarding my identity and who I choose to be, have I internalized and taken as my own?

THE IDENTITY JOURNAL

What day of the week is it?

What date and time is it?

Where am I?

Do you accept yourself for exactly who you are today?

THE IDENTITY JOURNAL

What day of the week is it?

What date and time is it?

Where am I?

Where is it in my life that I am seeking the most validation?

THE IDENTITY JOURNAL

What day of the week is it?

What date and time is it?

Where am I?

Who am I seeking or aiming to please in life, the full sum of me or the opinions of others?

THE IDENTITY JOURNAL

Time for the Daily Self-Acceptance Experience!

On the next several pages

You will utilize this space in time to create a positive dialogue for yourself

Telling yourself what you love most about yourself as many times as you want to

Come to this part of the journal when you feel the need to validate who you are

Go ahead and tell yourself the truth!

THE IDENTITY JOURNAL
Daily Self-Acceptance Experience!

THE IDENTITY JOURNAL

Daily Self-Acceptance Experience!

THE IDENTITY JOURNAL
Daily Self-Acceptance Experience!

THE IDENTITY JOURNAL

Daily Self-Acceptance Experience!

THE IDENTITY JOURNAL
Daily Self-Acceptance Experience!

THE IDENTITY JOURNAL
Daily Self-Acceptance Experience!

THE IDENTITY JOURNAL
Daily Self-Acceptance Experience!

THE IDENTITY JOURNAL

Daily Self-Acceptance Experience!

THE IDENTITY JOURNAL
Daily Self-Acceptance Experience!

THE IDENTITY JOURNAL

Daily Self-Acceptance Experience!

THE IDENTITY JOURNAL
Daily Self-Acceptance Experience!

THE IDENTITY JOURNAL

Daily Self-Acceptance Experience!

THE IDENTITY JOURNAL
Daily Self-Acceptance Experience!

THE IDENTITY JOURNAL
Daily Self-Acceptance Experience!

THE IDENTITY JOURNAL
Daily Self-Acceptance Experience!

THE IDENTITY JOURNAL
Daily Self-Acceptance Experience!

THE IDENTITY JOURNAL
Daily Self-Acceptance Experience!

THE IDENTITY JOURNAL
Daily Self-Acceptance Experience!

THE IDENTITY JOURNAL
Daily Self-Acceptance Experience!

THE IDENTITY JOURNAL
Daily Self-Acceptance Experience!

THE IDENTITY JOURNAL
Daily Self-Acceptance Experience!

THE IDENTITY JOURNAL
Daily Self-Acceptance Experience!

THE IDENTITY JOURNAL
Daily Self-Acceptance Experience!

THE IDENTITY JOURNAL
Daily Self-Acceptance Experience!

THE IDENTITY JOURNAL
Daily Self-Acceptance Experience!

THE IDENTITY JOURNAL
Daily Self-Acceptance Experience!

THE IDENTITY JOURNAL
Daily Self-Acceptance Experience!

THE IDENTITY JOURNAL
Daily Self-Acceptance Experience!

THE IDENTITY JOURNAL
Daily Self-Acceptance Experience!

THE IDENTITY JOURNAL
Daily Self-Acceptance Experience!

THE IDENTITY JOURNAL
Daily Self-Acceptance Experience!

THE IDENTITY JOURNAL
Daily Self-Acceptance Experience!

THE IDENTITY JOURNAL
Daily Self-Acceptance Experience!

THE IDENTITY JOURNAL
Daily Self-Acceptance Experience!

THE IDENTITY JOURNAL
Daily Self-Acceptance Experience!

THE IDENTITY JOURNAL
Daily Self-Acceptance Experience!

THE IDENTITY JOURNAL
Daily Self-Acceptance Experience!

THE IDENTITY JOURNAL
Daily Self-Acceptance Experience!

THE IDENTITY JOURNAL
Daily Self-Acceptance Experience!

Well this wraps up The Identity Journal!

Keep up the Journaling

and

Keep reaching for the truth regarding yourself and your ongoing healing, growth, and oneness with self!

THE IDENTITY JOURNAL

Other Books by the Author include:

Wisdom of the First Pure: The Journey Back to the 6th Dimension
Edition 1

Part One
Wisdom of the First Pure: The Journey back to the 6th Dimension
The Workbook
Edition 1

Excerpts from Exclaims of Sorrow: A Thirty Day Devotional Journey for the Relinquishment of Spiritual Pain

Wisdom of the First Pure: The Journey Back to the 6th Dimension

Part One

*The Revised Edition
Edition 2

THE IDENTITY JOURNAL

"You must hope in your own will power and own self-awareness of the fact that you alone are worthwhile. You, all by yourself, are worth spending the necessary time with yourself that is required to heal the pain." - Dr. Sonny Alonzo Dotson

Made in United States
North Haven, CT
06 February 2025